CODEX™

ORKS™

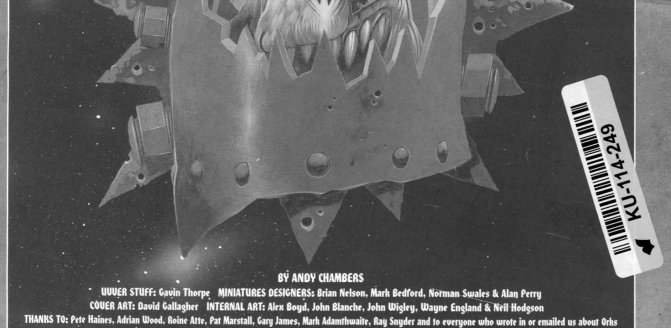

BY ANDY CHAMBERS

UUUER STUFF: Gavin Thorpe   MINIATURES DESIGNERS: Brian Nelson, Mark Bedford, Norman Swales & Alan Perry

COUER ART: David Gallagher   INTERNAL ART: Alex Boyd, John Blanche, John Wigley, Wayne England & Neil Hodgson

THANKS TO: Pete Haines, Adrian Wood, Roine Atte, Pat Marstall, Gary James, Mark Adamthwaite, Ray Snyder and to everyone who wrote in or emailed us about Orks

PRODUCED BY GAMES WORKSHOP

UK	US	AUSTRALIA	CANADA	HONG KONG
GAMES WORKSHOP LTD.	GAMES WORKSHOP INC.	GAMES WORKSHOP,	GAMES WORKSHOP,	GAMES WORKSHOP,
WILLOW RD, LENTON,	6721 BAYMEADOW DRIVE,	23 LIVERPOOL ST,	1645 BONHILL RD,	20th FLOOR,
NOTTINGHAM,	GLEN BURNIE,	INGLEBURN,	UNITS 9-11, MISSISSAUGA,	LEADER CENTRE,
NG7 2WS	MARYLAND, 21060 6401	NSW 2565	TORONTO L5T 1R3	37 WONG CHUK HANG ROAD

PRODUCT CODE: 60 03 01 03 002   Games Workshop World Wide Web site: http://www.games-workshop.com   ISBN: 1 869893 38 7

INTRODUCTION

Greetings Warboss, welcome to *Codex: Orks*, a book dedicated to collecting, painting and gaming with an Ork warband in the Warhammer 40,000 battle game. The Ork way is brutal and savage, using sledge-hammer tactics coupled with the ferocity of a bag of wolverines. If you're looking for the Warhammer 40,000 equivalent of a barbarian horde you're in the right place!

ORKS

Orks are the most widespread and warlike race of aliens in the bloodstained galaxy of the 41st millennium. From the depths of the core to the distant ghost stars beyond the galactic rim burgeoning Ork empires rise and fall. In terms of sheer numbers and planets Orks occupy more of the galaxy than any other single race and were they unified they would soon crush all opposition. However the Orks' passion for violence is so unquenchable that they spend most of their time warring amongst themselves and any Ork leader worth his followers' respect would never dream of voluntarily following another. But once in a generation an Ork leader will emerge who is powerful enough to defeat his rivals and dominate their tribes. His success will draw others and soon a great Ork Waaagh! is underway, a movement of millions; part migration, part holy jihad as the Orks seek

new worlds to conquer and races to enslave. The violence of Ork warriors unleashed is truly terrifying and the ferocity of the Ork Waaagh! evokes fear even amidst the holy spires of Terra.

WHY COLLECT AN ORK ARMY?

First off because Orks can fight anyone, even other Orks! No matter who your opponent is you can fight them with no qualms about whether you've got a realistic match-up. In the Warhammer 40,000 background Orks are the classic antagonists, a constant threat to all other races and are in a permanent state of war.

Orks are also an ideal army for the player who wants to field everything at once. Individual Orks are tough, capable warriors and mercifully cheap in points, so an Ork force can field a solid body of troops and still have plenty of room left to include warbikes, big guns, Dreadnoughts and other nasties. In battle the Ork army is a real horde, a solid mass of troops and vehicles which will make even the most hardened Space Marines player balk.

The Orks themselves are excellent hand-to-hand fighters. Even the most basically equipped Ork fights better in close combat than many races' assault specialists, and a whole mob of Orks can overrun most enemy units with ease. Better still, the Orks' confidence in their own fighting abilities means that mobs have to be decimated before they even think about retreating and Orks which do fall back are likely to join up with another mob and renew the attack. This makes the Orks' brutal style of combat easy to emulate on the tabletop, and even if they lose you can win a moral victory if you have the right sense of bravado and mutter things like "You haven't heard the last of us, meddling Space Marine!".

Ork barbarity is also highly entertaining in itself. If you want a straight laced army that takes itself seriously try the Eldar or Sisters of Battle! A good Ork player can have a laugh at the expense of his Gretchin slaves getting blown to bits when they're sent into a minefield, or when one of the Mekboyz' insane weapons blows up or a supercharged vehicle smashes into a wall.

The crude, barbaric style of an Ork army lends itself well to painters more interested in fielding a big force than an immaculately painted one. By using basic painting techniques an Ork force can be easily assembled, with its sheer mass of warriors compensating for their individual simplicity. Nearly everything the Orks use is hand built and heavily personalised, be it weapons, armour, vehicles or bioniks. This offers modellers a vast range of possibilities for converting and scratch building, making Ork armies the most varied, individualistic creations in the Warhammer 40,000 game.

Sir, despite repeated efforts at alerting sector command to the alien threat emanating from the Alacanth, Redwold and Tyr systems no action has been undertaken. Naval scouting forces have noted a sharp increase in the build-up of Ork ships within these systems and the recent loss of the Falchion class cruiser Tempest in the Tyr system has rendered further reconnaissance impossible. It is imperative that further information is gathered by whatever means possible to ensure the continued security of the Kolchis system. >>>>>>>>>>>>>>>

Date: 2763994.M41

Sir, my thanks for the recent intelligence on Ork activity in the sub-sector. This, combined with my own sources, makes it clear that an Ork Waaagh is imminent. The central figure appears to be Warlord Gorbad of the Redskulls tribe. Gorbad has conquered all neighbouring tribes on Redwold, Tyr and Alacanth over the last four years and is now building heavy armaments and invasion ships. Rumours abound of two (or more) space hulks being sighted in the Redwold system and the Emperor's Tarot produces ever more dire portents of strife. I would suggest, nay, request that a pre-emptive strike be made on Redwold to cripple the Ork's shipping and eliminate their leader before this dangerous situation gets further out of hand. I would also note that the Angels of Absolution have recently fought on Belami and would make an eminently suitable strike force. >>>>>>>>>>

Date: 2800994.M41

Sir, I find it inconceivable that slaying the Ork's leader would not result in the dissipation of the Waaagh. You assure me that another Warlord would simply take his place, but surely a period of internecine warfare would occur as his rivals fought to take control? I only pray that the Angels of Absolution will undertake to raid on our behalf. >>>>>>>>>>>>>>>>>

Date: 2851994.M41

The outer early warning beacons have detected an alien fleet moving into the Kolchis system. Patrol ships have been dispatched to investigate and planetary defence forces have been placed on full alert. >>

Date: 2967994.M41

The Ork fleet of Waaagh Gorbad has breached our orbital defences and even now Ork attack ships and assault boats are landing forces on the planet. Fast-moving spearheads have isolated the capital from the outer mines. Early estimates place the attacking ground forces at the equivalent of sixteen regiments, with one hulk, four cruisers and twenty plus attack ships supporting from orbit. >>>>>>>>>>>>>>>>>>>>>>>>>>>>>>>>>>>>>

Date: 2093995.M41

All outer defences overrun. Orks are engaged in street fighting throughout the capital. Supplies running low and fighting forces shattered. Collapse of all resistance estimated at six days maximum.

Commend our souls to the Emperor. >>>

<<<<<< NO FURTHER TRANSMISSIONS >>>>>>

Transmitted: Kolchis
Received: Ryza
Telepathic Duct:
Astropath-Terminus Sondavi
Author: Commander Heironys
Date: 4255994.M41

Transmission intercepted at Inquisition station 574363/b/Mk3.

Addenda: Full transcript suppressed for reasons of Sector security by order of Inquisitor Marles. Full transcript available via archive Xeno. Arc/u.i.s/897.delta Security clearance Vermillion. Cross-ref: Angels of Absolution. Belami Incursion. Waaagh Gorbad. Warlord Gorbad. Redwold. Alacanth. Tyr. Ryza.

Appended note by Inquisitor Marles: The sacrifice of Kolchis has given Ryza an additional seven month build-up, somewhat less than the period required by Solar Hostarax but greater than would have been gained by prematurely instigating the Waaagh by taking action. Exhaustion of the Kolchis mines was estimated within twelve standard years.

And at this time
the brazen god of war
cast up a great lord
to lead the savages forth

The Book of War

This section of *Codex: Orks* contains information on the different troops and vehicles an Ork Warboss (ie YOU!) can use. The list allows you to fight battles using the scenarios included in the Warhammer 40,000 rulebook, but also provides the basic information you'll need to field an Ork army in scenarios you've devised yourself, or that form part of a campaign.

The army list is split into five sections. All squads, vehicles and characters in the army list are placed into one of these sections, depending upon their role on the battlefield: *Headquarters (HQ), Elites, Troops, Fast Attack* and *Heavy Support*. Every model included in the army list also has a points value, which varies depending on how effective it is on the battlefield.

Before you can choose an army for a battle you will need to agree with your opponent upon what scenario to play and the points each of you have to spend on your army. Having done this you can proceed to pick an army as described below.

USING A FORCE ORGANISATION CHART

The army list is used with the force organisation charts from a scenario. Each chart is split into five categories that correspond to the sections in the army list, and each category may have one or more boxes. Each light-toned box indicates that you *may* make one choice from that section of the army list, while a dark-toned box means that you *must* make a choice from that section.

Note that unless a model or vehicle forms part of a squad or a squadron it counts as a single choice from those available to your army.

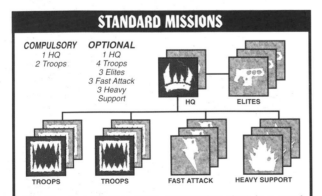

STANDARD MISSIONS

COMPULSORY	OPTIONAL
1 HQ	1 HQ
2 Troops	4 Troops
	3 Elites
	3 Fast Attack
	3 Heavy Support

*The Standard Missions force organisation chart is a good example of how to choose an army. To begin with you will need at least one HQ unit and two Troop units (dark shaded boxes indicate units that **must** be taken for the mission). This leaves the following for you to choose from to make up your army's total points value: up to 1 HQ unit, 0-3 additional Elite units, 0-4 additional Troop units, 0-3 additional Fast Attack units or 0-3 additional Heavy Support units.*

USING THE ARMY LISTS

To make a choice, look in the relevant section of the army list and decide what unit you wish to have in your army, how many models there will be in it, and which upgrades you want (if any). Remember you <u>cannot</u> field models that are equipped with weapons and wargear not shown on the model. Once this is done subtract the points value of the unit from your total points, and then go back and make another choice. Continue doing this until you have used up all your points. Then you can get on with the serious business of unleashing your deadly Ork Waaagh!

ARMY LIST ENTRIES

Each army list entry consists of the following:

Unit Name: The type of unit and any limitations on the maximum number of choices you can make for that unit type (0-1, for example, indicates that only one unit may be included in the army).

Profile: These are the characteristics of that unit type, including its points cost. Where the unit contains different warriors, there may be more than one profile.

Number/Squad: The number of models allowed in the unit, or the number of models you may take for one choice from the force organisation chart. Often this is a variable amount, in which case it shows the minimum and maximum unit size.

Weapons: These are the unit's standard weapons.

Options: Lists the different weapon and equipment options for the unit and any additional points for taking these options. It may also include the option to upgrade one mob member to a character. If a mob is allowed to have models with upgraded weaponry (such as big shootas or rokkit launchas), then these must be given to ordinary squad members, not the character.

Special Rules: This is where you'll find any special rules that apply to the unit.

ORK SPECIAL RULES

The following special rules apply to all Ork units except where noted.

MIXED ARMOUR

Due to the wide variety of wargear and the Ork Mobbing Up rule it is entirely possible for some units to include models with different armour saves. Because of this the normal casualty removal and armour save rules are altered slightly.

The opposing player rolls to hit and wound for whichever unit he is firing with as normal. However, when the Ork player makes armour saves before removing casualties from a unit that has mixed armour saves he uses the best armour saves as long as the Orks wearing that type of armour are in the majority (ie, they outnumber Orks with worse saves in the unit). This represents the heavily armoured Orks making more obvious targets and the lighter armoured Orks using them as cover! Any casualties removed after saving throws have been taken must come from amongst the most heavily armoured Orks first (ie, the ones with the best saving throws take the hits).

If heavier armoured Orks are in the minority use the worse armour saves and take the casualties from the lightly armoured Orks instead.

For example: A Warboss and his bodyguard of five Nobz suffer 6 wounds from enemy fire. The Warboss and three of his bodyguard are wearing mega armour so the Ork player rolls his saving throws using the 2+ mega armour save (as the models with mega armour outnumber the other models in the mob). Unluckily he fails two saves and 2 wounds are suffered. Because the Nobz have 2 wounds each, one mega armoured Nob is removed as a casualty. If the enemy fire had an Armour Penetration of 2 or better, three mega armoured Nobz would be removed as casualties (ouch!).

ORK MOB RULE!

An Ork mob has to check morale and test for pinning from barrages and snipers in the same way as any other unit. However, if the mob fails a test it will immediately 'check size' by rolling 2D6. If the score is equal to or less than the number of Orks (not including Gretchin) left in the mob then the Orks carry on, confident in the belief there are enough of them left to win. Their courage is bolstered by their comrades, spurring them on to battle. This means that an Ork mob of twelve models or more will always fight on, regardless of any casualties it might have received.

Mobbing Up

Orks falling back can attempt to regroup as normal if there are enough of them left, but this rarely happens as Orks will only withdraw once most of them are dead. However, an Ork unit of any size can attempt to join another mob or in other words 'mob up'.

When Orks fall back they can move towards any Ork mob that lies behind their own position. If any withdrawing Orks get within 6" of the new mob once moves are complete then the withdrawing mob can attempt to join up with the new one. Make a 2D6 roll against the Leadership value of the mob which is falling back. If successful the two mobs combine together (mob up) and the previously withdrawing mob can immediately move up to 6" so they are in proper formation.

Only Ork foot troops will mob up in this way – Slavers and Meks in charge of Grot mobs or Big Gunz, Stormboyz and warbikes may not mob up.

Victory Points after Mobbing Up

A mob of Orks which mobs up counts as destroyed for victory points purposes. An Ork mob which gains additional Orks from another mob joining up with them is not worth any more victory points than it was before, it will still use its starting strength and points value for working out victory points.

THE POWER OF THE WAAAGH!

When a big mob of Orks charges they form a solid mass, blazing away with their shootas and screaming Waaagh! at the top of their lungs. The sheer momentum of their charge is stunning and opponents are in danger of getting bowled over by a scrum of Orks all trying to get into combat first.

To represent the Power of the Waaagh!, when an Ork mob charges into close combat check its size by rolling 2D6. If the score is equal to or under the number of Orks left in the mob they charge in with a rousing "Waaaaaaaaagh!". All the Orks in the mob double their Initiative characteristic for the rest of the assault phase. In future assault phases the Orks revert to their normal Initiative values. If the 2D6 roll is greater than the number of Orks left in the mob the Orks charge in as normal and attack with their basic Initiative value.

Orks who make a sweeping advance into the enemy also use the Power of the Waaagh! The test for this is made at the beginning of the assault phase so any casualties from enemy fire will reduce the chances of them managing to maintain their momentum.

> He was an avalanche from an unexpected quarter. He was a thunderbolt from a clear sky.
>
> Commissar Yarrick on Ghazghkull Thraka.

GRETCHIN MOBS

Gretchin are notoriously cowardly by Ork standards so in battle they are led (or rather driven forward) by an Ork Slaver. In the case of these units Morale checks are made against the Ork's Leadership value – but there is no Mob Rule for Gretchin. Grotz don't count when it comes to counting heads!

Gretchin are affected by Morale checks for losing an assault just like normal troops. However, Gretchin who fail a Morale check caused by enemy shooting or tank shock or which fail to regroup after falling back from close combat, 'go to ground' and hide with almost preternatural skill; in the blink of an eye they disappear under rocks, behind foliage, and whatever else they can hide in. The Gretchin mob is removed and the Slaver is left in place to indicate their position (as he starts the thankless task of rounding them up again). If no Slaver is present (ie, he has been slain or was not included in the mob for some reason) the Gretchin mob may not regroup and counts as being destroyed.

Gretchin can attempt to regroup each turn as long as the Slaver is still alive, even if the Gretchin mob has been reduced below 50% of its original strength or the enemy is within 6". If the Gretchin have gone into hiding, when they regroup they are replaced on the tabletop in coherency with the Slaver but not more than 6" from him. Whilst they are hiding Gretchin cannot be harmed.

Ork Slaverz trying to regroup Gretchin can be attacked as normal by shooting and in close combat. The Slaver may not move, shoot or initiate an assault (although he can still fight back if attacked in close combat). If the Slaver is killed the Gretchin mob counts as being destroyed.

ORK ARMOURY

In most cases characters are upgraded from ordinary Boyz. Where this is the case the character keeps the basic weapons and wargear of the mob he's part of – for example, a Stormboyz Nob has a slugga, choppa and jump pack. This doesn't prevent you from picking extra weapons for him from the Armoury although the restrictions on the number of weapons that can be carried always apply.

Ork characters may have up to two single-handed weapons, or one single-handed weapon and one two-handed weapon. You may also pick up to 40 points of extra wargear for each character from the Wargear lists (80 points for an Ork Warboss and 60 points for a Big Mek or Painboss). The full Wargear rules are on pages 34-37. You can not take duplicate items for the same model with the exception of Grots or squigs and all wargear and weapons must be represented on the model.

SINGLE HANDED WEAPONS

Choppa	2 pts
Power claw	25 pts
Slugga	1 pt
'Urty syringe (Mad Doks only)	5 pts

TWO-HANDED WEAPONS

Big shoota	12 pts
Burna (Mekboyz only)	10 pts
Grabba stik (Slaverz only)	5 pts
Kombi weapon: shoota/rokkit launcha	5 pts
Kombi weapon: shoota/skorcha	8 pts
Kustom force field (Mekboyz only)	20 pts
Kustom mega-blasta (Mekboyz only)	15 pts
Rokkit launcha	8 pts
Shoota	2 pts
'Uge choppa	10 pts

ORK VEHICLE UPGRADES

Any Ork vehicles (apart from warbikes) may be fitted with the following additional equipment. Any upgrades chosen must be shown on the vehicle model. Dreadnoughts may only choose upgrades marked with an (*). No duplicate upgrades may be taken for the same vehicle.

Armour plates*	5/10 pts
Big grabber	5 pts
Boarding plank	5 pts
Grot riggers	2 pts
Bolt-on big shoota (wartrukks only)	10 pts
Red paint job	3 pts
Reinforced ram	5 pts
Searchlight*	1 pt
Spikes 'n blades (not wartrukks)	5 pts
Stikkbomb chucka*	3 pts
Turbo boosta	5 pts
Wrecker ball	5 pts

WARGEAR

Ammo runt	4 pts
Attack squig	6 pts
Big horns/iron gob (Warboss & Nobz only)	6 pts
Bionik arm	10 pts
Bionik bonce	10 pts
Bosspole (Warboss & Nobz only)	3 pts
Cybork body	10 pts
Dok's tools (Mad Doks only)	1 pt
'Eavy armour	8 pts
Frag stikkbombz	1 pt
Grot oiler (Mekboyz only)	6 pts
Grot orderly (Mad Doks only)	6 pts
Krak stikkbombz	2 pts
Kustom job: More Dakka	4 pts
Blasta	3 pts
Shootier	2 pts
Mega armour (Warboss & Nobz only)	30 pts
Mega boosta (mega armour only)	10 pts
Mekboy's tools (Mekboyz only)	2 pts
Squighound (Slaverz only)	5 pts
Stikkbomb chucka (mega armour only)	1 pt
Super stikkbombz (Mekboyz only)	5 pts
Tankbusta bombz	3 pts
Waaagh! banner (max. one per army)	20 pts

Mega Armoured Warboss and Bodyguard

If an Ork Warboss is equipped with mega armour any members of his bodyguard Nobz that are also equipped with mega armour will be able choose up to a total of 80 points of wargear each (including the mega armour).

Grots and Squigs

Some Ork wargear takes the form of Gretchin slaves or squigs (short for 'squiggly beasts' – animals that Orks eat or train for simple tasks). Grot slaves and squigs must be represented by a separate model and become part of whichever mob the character they are with belongs to. They must also stay within the 2" coherency distance of the unit.

Note that the special rules for Grot morale only apply to mobs of the little green blighters, not to any Grots that are chosen as wargear. An Ork character may choose up to a maximum of three Grot slaves and/or squigs.

HEADQUARTERS

As the monstrous and all powerful leader of the warband the Warboss gets first pick of any wargear and the best fighters to make up his bodyguard with. Some Warbosses also include Mekboyz and Mad Doks in their bodyguard — often with their own small entourages of Grot slaves and squigs. Others just get in their wartrukks with a select band of hard nuts and lead their Boyz by the simple expedient of careering into the middle of the enemy force first!

WARBOSS

	Points	WS	BS	S	T	W	I	A	Ld	Sv
Warboss	60	5	2	5	4	3	4	4	9	6+

Your army must include a Warboss.

Options: A Warboss may be given any equipment allowed from the Ork Armoury.

Bodyguard: The Warboss may be accompanied by a bodyguard (see entry below). If he has a bodyguard then the Warboss and his bodyguard are treated as a single unit during battle. Note that the bodyguard does not count as a separate HQ choice (it does not use up a HQ 'slot').

Wartrukk: If the Warboss and his bodyguard number ten models or less (including squigs, Grots, etc) they may be mounted in a wartrukk at a cost of +30 pts. See below for details.

SPECIAL RULE

Independent Character: Unless accompanied by his bodyguard (see below) the Warboss is an independent character and follows all the rules for independent characters as given in the Warhammer 40,000 rulebook.

WARBOSS'S BODYGUARD

NOBZ

	Points/model	WS	BS	S	T	W	I	A	Ld	Sv
Nob	20	4	2	4	4	2	3	3	7	6+

Number: The Warboss may be accompanied by between five and ten Nobz.
Options: The Nobz may be given any equipment allowed from the Ork Armoury.

MEKBOYZ

	Points/model	WS	BS	S	T	W	I	A	Ld	Sv
Mekboy	10	4	2	3	4	1	2	2	7	6+

Number: If the Warboss is accompanied by a bodyguard he may also be accompanied by up to two Mekboyz.
Options: The Mekboyz may be given any equipment allowed from the Ork Armoury.

MAD DOKS

	Points/model	WS	BS	S	T	W	I	A	Ld	Sv
Mad Dok	10	4	2	3	4	1	2	2	7	6+

Number: If the Warboss is accompanied by a bodyguard he may also be accompanied by up to two Mad Doks.
Options: The Mad Doks may be given any equipment allowed from the Ork Armoury.

The wartrukk is a lightly armoured, fast transport vehicle used by Orks for getting the Boyz into battle quickly. It allows them to thrust deep into enemy lines and capture forward positions.

TRANSPORT: WARTRUKK

	Points	Front Armour	Side Armour	Rear Armour	BS
Wartrukk	30	10	10	10	2

Type: Fast, open topped. **Crew:** Orks.
Weapons: The wartrukk is armed with either a big shoota at +8 pts or a rokkit launcha at +5 pts.

O-I BIG MEK

	Points	WS	BS	S	T	W	I	A	Ld	Sv
Big Mek	25	4	2	4	4	2	3	3	7	6+

Options: A Big Mek may be given any equipment allowed from the Ork Armoury for Mekboyz, and also any equipment that can normally only be chosen by the Warboss and Nobz.

Bodyguard: The Big Mek may be accompanied by a bodyguard as detailed below. If the Big Mek has a bodyguard then he and the bodyguard are treated as a single unit during the battle. Note that the bodyguard does not count as a separate HQ choice (it does not use up one of the HQ 'slots').

Wartrukk: The Big Mek and his bodyguard may be mounted in a wartrukk at an additional cost of +30 pts. See the wartrukk entry on page 8 for details.

SPECIAL RULE

Independent Character: Unless accompanied by his bodyguard the Big Mek is an independent character and follows all of the rules for independent characters as given in the Warhammer 40,000 rulebook.

BIG MEK'S BODYGUARD

MEKBOYZ

	Points/model	WS	BS	S	T	W	I	A	Ld	Sv
Mekboy	10	4	2	3	4	1	2	2	7	6+

Number: The Big Mek may be accompanied by between three and five Mekboyz.

Options: The Mekboyz may be given any equipment allowed from the Ork Armoury. Mekboyz are highly individualistic and have a violent aversion to 'standardised' weapons. For this reason no Mekboyz in the bodyguard may be equipped with the same combination of weapons.

O-I PAINBOSS

	Points	WS	BS	S	T	W	I	A	Ld	Sv
Painboss	25	4	2	4	4	2	3	3	7	6+

Options: A Painboss may be given any equipment allowed for Mad Doks from the Ork Armoury.

Bodyguard: The Painboss may be accompanied by a bodyguard as detailed below. If he has a bodyguard then he and the bodyguard are treated as a single unit during battle. Note that the bodyguard does not count as a separate HQ choice (it does not use up a HQ 'slot').

Wartrukk: The Painboss and his bodyguard may be mounted in a wartrukk at an additional cost of +30 pts. See the wartrukk entry on page 8 for details.

SPECIAL RULE

Independent Character: Unless accompanied by his bodyguard the Painboss is an independent character and follows all of the rules for independent characters as given in the Warhammer 40,000 rulebook.

PAINBOSS'S BODYGUARD

CYBORKS

	Points/model	WS	BS	S	T	W	I	A	Ld	Sv
Cybork	13	4	2	4	5	1	2	2	7	5+

Number: The Painboss may be accompanied by between four and nine Cyborks.

Weapons: Sluggas and choppas.

Special Rule: The Cyborks have an invulnerable saving throw.

Occasionally a Mekboy will exhibit the kind of ambition usually only seen amongst Nobz. Although he can never aspire to lead a whole warband the Mekboy will gather other Mekboyz as followers and gain in power and stature. It is common for a Big Mek to leave his warband or be outlawed by its Warboss for getting too big for his boots. Outlaw Big Meks and their followers will hire out their services to warbands, searching for a war big enough to satisfy their obsession for building the biggest, shootiest war machines around.

Veteran Painboyz become increasingly obsessed with perfecting their own methods of 'serjery' and eventually drift away from their Warboss. Left to their own devices, they will indulge in ever more extreme eksperiments. Any Ork brave/stupid enough to venture into a Painboss's lab has to be careful otherwise it may wake up to find itself with a new set of mechanical lungs that allow it to breathe underwater even though it probably only went in to get a bad tooth removed!

ELITES

Stormboyz are fierce Ork warriors who are willing to gamble with their lives (and their sanity) by strapping on crude Ork rokkit packs to blast them towards the enemy.

STORMBOYZ										
	Points/model	WS	BS	S	T	W	I	A	Ld	Sv
Boyz	15	4	2	3	4	1	2	2	7	6+
Nob	+11	4	2	4	4	2	3	3	7	6+

Mob: The mob consists of between five and twenty Ork Stormboyz.

Weapons: Sluggas and choppas.

Options: The entire mob may be equipped with frag stikkbombz at +1 pt per model and krak stikkbombz at +2 pts per model.

Character: For an additional cost of +11 pts one of the Stormboyz may be upgraded to a Nob. The Nob may be given any equipment allowed from the Ork Armoury, except mega armour.

SPECIAL RULE

Jump Packs: The mob is equipped with jump packs. See the Warhammer 40,000 rulebook for details.

Kommandos are the most slippery, cunning and untrustworthy Orks in any warband. On the other hand they are the best at slithering closer to an enemy battleline or sneaking around a flank without raising the alarm.

KOMMANDOS										
	Points/model	WS	BS	S	T	W	I	A	Ld	Sv
Boyz	10	4	2	3	4	1	2	2	7	–
Nob	+11	4	2	4	4	2	3	3	7	–

Mob: The mob consists of between five and ten Kommandos.

Weapons: The models in the mob may be armed with either a shoota or slugga & choppa (you may have a mixture of weapons within the mob).

Options: Up to one model in the mob can be armed with either a big shoota at +8 pts, rokkit launcha at +5 pts or burna at +6 pts. The mob may have frag stikkbombz at +1 pt per model, krak stikkbombz at +2 pts per model and/or tankbusta bombz at +3 pts per model.

Character: For an additional cost of +11 pts one of the Kommandos may be upgraded to a Nob. The Nob is allowed to have any equipment allowed from the Ork Armoury, except for mega armour.

SPECIAL RULES

Infiltrators: Kommandos are Infiltrators and follow any special scenario rules for Infiltrators.

Slippery: Kommandos sneak through cover quickly and easily, so they roll an extra D6 when they move through difficult ground.

'Ard Boyz wear heavy armour pieced together from steel plates and equipment scavenged from defeated foes. Their thick armour combined with the natural toughness of Orks means that 'Ard Boyz are able to wade through the fiercest fire fights with barely a scratch.

'ARD BOYZ										
	Points/model	WS	BS	S	T	W	I	A	Ld	Sv
Boyz	12	4	2	3	4	1	2	2	7	4+
Nob	+16	4	2	4	4	2	3	3	7	4+

Mob: The mob consists of between five and twenty 'Ard Boyz

Weapons: The models in the mob may be armed with either a shoota or slugga & choppa (you may have a mixture of weapons within the mob).

Options: Up to three models in the mob can be armed with either a big shoota at +8 pts, a rokkit launcha at +5 pts or a burna at +6 pts. The entire mob may be equipped with frag stikkbombz at +1 pts per model, and/or krak stikkbombz at +2 pts per model.

Character: For an additional cost of +16 pts one of the Boyz may be upgraded to a Nob. The Nob may be given any additional equipment allowed from the Ork Armoury.

SKARBOYZ										
	Points/model	WS	BS	S	T	W	I	A	Ld	Sv
Boyz	11	4	2	4	4	1	2	2	7	6+
Nob	+9	4	2	4	4	2	3	3	7	6+

Mob: The mob consists of between five and twenty Skarboyz.

Weapons: The models in the mob may be armed with either a shoota or slugga & choppa (you may have a mixture of weapons within the mob).

Options: Up to three models in the mob can be armed with either a big shoota at +8 pts, a rokkit launcha at +5 pts or a burna at +8 pts. The entire mob may be equipped with frag stikkbombz at +1 pt per model, krak stikkbombz at +2 pts per model.

Character: For an additional cost of +9 pts one of the Boyz may be upgraded to a Nob. The Nob may be given any additional equipment allowed from the Ork Armoury.

Skarboyz are veteran warriors who bear the scars of dozens of battles. These Orks have grown exceptionally big and strong and have brawny, gnarled arms bulging with slabs of muscle from fighting in numerous conflicts.

0-1 FLASH GITZ										
	Points/model	WS	BS	S	T	W	I	A	Ld	Sv
Boyz	9	4	2	3	4	1	2	2	7	6+
Nob	+11	4	2	4	4	2	3	3	7	6+

Mob: The mob consists of between five and twenty Flash Gitz.

Weapons: Shoota.

Options: The entire mob may be given one kustom job for their shootas chosen from the Wargear section: *Shootier:* +2 pts per model, *Blasta:* +3 pts per model and *More Dakka:* +4 pts per model. Up to four models can have either a big shoota at +8 pts, a rokkit launcha at +5 pts or a burna at +6 pts.

Character: For an additional cost of +11 pts one of the Gitz may be upgraded to a Nob. The Nob may be given any equipment allowed from the Ork Armoury.

Some Orks are so obsessed with guns that they will scrape together all the wealth they can to get the best kustom shoota they can afford. Other Orks call these over-equipped nuttas 'Flash Gitz'.

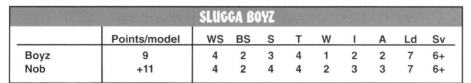

TROOPS

SLUGGA BOYZ										
	Points/model	WS	BS	S	T	W	I	A	Ld	Sv
Boyz	9	4	2	3	4	1	2	2	7	6+
Nob	+11	4	2	4	4	2	3	3	7	6+

Mob: The mob consists of between ten and thirty Boyz.

Weapons: Slugga and choppa.

Options: Up to three models can have either a big shoota at +8 pts, a rokkit launcha at +5 pts or a burna at +6 pts.

Character: For an additional cost of +11 pts one of the Boyz may be upgraded to a Nob. The Nob may be given any equipment allowed by the Ork Armoury.

Slugga Boyz are the heart and soul of most Ork warbands. They are normally formed into huge mobs and are armed for close combat with hefty, razor-edged choppas and the big-bore Ork pistols known as sluggas.

SHOOTA BOYZ										
	Points/model	WS	BS	S	T	W	I	A	Ld	Sv
Boyz	8	4	2	3	4	1	2	2	7	6+
Nob	+12	4	2	4	4	2	3	3	7	6+

Mob: The mob consists of between ten and thirty Shoota Boyz.

Weapons: Shoota.

Options: Up to three models can have either a big shoota at +8 pts, rokkit launcha at +5 pts or burna at +6 pts.

Character: For an extra +12 pts one Boy may be upgraded to a Nob and given any equipment allowed from the Ork Armoury.

The deafening clamour of a mob of Shoota Boyz opening fire is legendary. Each Ork will try to outdo his neighbour by letting fly with the most ammo and the loudest gun. Hitting the target is less of an objective than terrorising the enemy!

WHAT'S IN THE ARMY?

Da Boyz form the heart of an Ork army, constituting the ferocious mass of warriors it needs to win a battle. All Ork Boyz excel in close combat and the more Boyz that get stuck in the better! Using big mobs of Orks is important because it stops their assaults being broken up by enemy fire. Specialist Orks such as Tankbustas and Burna Boyz should be used for tackling important objectives or especially tough enemies.

Da Wheelz give an Ork army mobility and firepower but are vulnerable to enemy shooting. They are best used in support of the main advance, pinning down an enemy and distracting them while Da Boyz close in to attack.

Da 'Ard Stuff has thick armour, powerful weaponry and inflicts tremendous carnage in assaults. If Da 'Ard Stuff attacks alongside Da Boyz the enemy can be forced to divide their firing, giving both elements a good chance of survival.

Da Big Gunz give supporting fire so that the most dangerous enemy units can be blasted to bits at long range. Big Gunz are vulnerable to enemy shooting and assaults so they need to be placed where they will be protected by other mobs.

EXPANDING YOUR ARMY

Adrian Wood's Waaagh! Grishnak.

Andy: Armed with your Warboss and two Troops units you have a core force for your army. However, you'll soon want to expand it by adding new units, though deciding exactly what to add can be a tough choice. The approach I find best is to add in one unit from each category which you don't already have – a Fast Attack unit, a Heavy Support unit and an Elite unit. At this stage it will be useful to try out these different parts of the army and see which suits your tactics best. Later you may decide to add more choices from one or other of these categories based on your experience in games, or you may want to add more Troops instead, but having a bit of each to begin with will be a useful way to start learning how your army works.

To give you some helpful pointers we've included two armies collected by experienced Greenskins, Adrian 'Grand Warlord' Wood and myself. As you can see, both armies include a powerful core force of Boyz, but there the similarities end. Adrian has a lot of Wheelz in his army (Fast Attack choices, that is) because experience has taught him to move quickly to pin down the enemy. I, on the other hand, have gone for more Big Gunz and 'Ard Stuff (Heavy Support) to try and land a 'knock out punch' which will send the enemy reeling if it connects! The mark of an Ork army is the endless variety of miniatures, so both armies contain loads of great conversions.

Andy Chambers' Blitz Boyz

19

ORK TACTICS

On this page are some different battle plans for an Ork army. These are just the basic ideas, and leave plenty of room for you to tailor these tactics to your own forces and different opponents.

Wartrak Rumble

Dread Bash

WARTRAK RUMBLE

The *Wartrak Rumble* works well if you have a lot of Wheelz – trukks, wartraks, buggies and warbikes – in your force. Mass all of your Wheelz on one side of the battlefield, preferably one that has lots of terrain to block off the enemy's lines of fire to them. As Da Boyz advance, Da Wheelz race around to attack the rear of the enemy battle line, catching the enemy forces between the 'hammer' of Da Wheelz and the 'anvil' of Da Boyz (Adrian Wood calls this the 'Gorka Morka' after the Orkish gods of violence and cunning).

DREAD BASH

The *Dread Bash* uses a powerful force of 'Ard Stuff – Ork Dreadnoughts and Killer Kans – to give an armoured spearhead to Da Boyz' attack. Deploy your 'Ard Stuff along a short part of your battle line, backed up by your toughest mobs of Boyz. As with the *Wartrak Rumble*, try to use any available terrain to cut down on the amount of incoming enemy fire as your force advances, but don't hide or dawdle, close in quick! Use your 'Ard Stuff to tear a hole in the enemy forces so that Da Boyz can pour in and start destroying their battle line.

SWAMP 'EM

When you *Swamp 'Em* you need a force made up mostly of Da Boyz and loads of Gretchin slaves. Deploy Da Boyz across a broad front and place the Gretchin out in front as cannon fodder, but have one or two units of Boyz behind the line so that other Orks which fall back can mob up with them. The enemy should have too many targets to be able to stop them all with shooting, so you will start to overrun his battle line in several places. The mobs furthest back will then arrive, reinforced by Orks which have mobbed up with them, and finish off any pockets of resistance.

Swamp 'Em

PAINTING ORKS

So your head's full of cunnin' plans on how to crush your foes, but what about painting all those greenskin warriors? In this section we'll impart some of the tricks of the trade when it comes to painting Orks.

ORK SKIN

Goblin Green drybrushed over Dark Angels Green, followed by a mix of Goblin Green and Bleached Bone drybrushed on as a highlight.

Painting Ork skin is the most important thing in creating an impressive Ork army.

There are as many ways of painting Ork skin as there are Ork gamers and each one has their own style. Some like to paint their Orks simply, so they can paint lots at the same time. Others prefer to carefully highlight and shade their models for maximum effect. Whichever way you paint your Orks, bear in mind that you will be painting dozens of them, so choose a style that allows you to paint lots of models easily. A single coat of Goblin Green on a mass of Ork Boyz looks fine.

There are a few simple tricks you can use to add more detail to your models. For example, a wash

Goblin Green washed with Green ink then drybrushed with a mix of Goblin Green and Bleached Bone as a highlight.

of Green ink will add instant shading to your Boyz. Another trick is to drybrush on a lighter green to highlight the detail. We've included some examples of painting Ork flesh on this page, but you can use all sorts of combinations of Green ink wash and different colours for highlighting. Feel free to experiment.

Gretchin and Nobz can be painted differently to Ork Boyz. This Grot has been painted with a mix of Goblin Green and Bleached Bone to make it paler and weaker-looking than Da Boyz.

Goblin Green, this time painted over Dark Angels Green and then highlighted with a mix of Goblin Green and Bleached Bone.

Many painters prefer to paint Nobz a much darker tone than Boyz to signify their age and strength – simply leave off the highlighting stage or use darker colours.

PAINTING METAL

Use Boltgun Metal to paint your guns and choppas. It that looks good after a single coat and can be highlighted with Chainmail. A wash of Rust Brown ink will make your guns look weather-worn. In comparison, Tin Bitz is a much darker and browner metal colour. Used as a base colour and highlighted with Boltgun Metal, you get even dirtier looking guns.

TEETH

You can paint teeth and horns with Bleached Bone – a couple of coats will look good even over black. If you want your model's teeth to look more discoloured, use a wash of Rust Brown ink. You can also use Bubonic Brown or Codex Grey as a base colour for teeth. We painted the horns on this Nob with Scorched Brown first, then the ridges were painted on with Bubonic Brown and then Bleached Bone.

DRYBRUSHING

One way to paint Orks is to drybrush them, which is a way of highlighting models, particularly if they have textured surfaces. Start with your base colour and either lighten it with Skull White or choose a lighter version of it (eg, Bleached Bone is a lighter version of Bubonic Brown). Wipe away most of the paint on a tissue and lightly brush over the raised areas of the miniature. The colour in the brush will come off onto the detail, highlighting it. The more you drybrush over the model, the lighter the model will look, so you can easily vary the look of all your models within a mob. You can paint armour, fur, vehicles and Ork skin this way if you like.

◀ *This is the end result of Adrian drybrushing over Dark Angels Green as discussed above.*

The skin of these Orks (painted by Adrian Wood) has been drybrushed – the muscles particularly suit this style of painting. The skin was first painted a base colour of Dark Angels Green and was then drybrushed with a mix of Dark Angels Green and Goblin Green. Adrian then drybrushed the whole model with Goblin Green followed by a mix of Goblin Green and Rotting Flesh. Finally the model had the lightest drybrushing of Rotting Flesh. Excessive, but it looks good!

To make the shading look nice and crisp Adrian painted on final highlights with a mix of Goblin Green and Rotting Flesh.

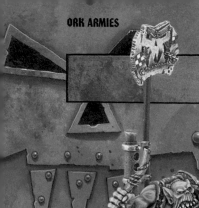

THE ORK CLANZ

Ork warbands often belong to a specific Ork clan which has its own colour schemes, glyphs and markings. On the next few pages you can see examples of these that you can use to paint your army…

GOFFS

Goff clan Orks think they are the toughest, most no-nonsense warriors around and wear a uniform that is sombre black with some white and red detailing. Black and white checks are especially popular.

Nob with power claw and bosspole.

This war buggy is equipped with a ram.

Shoota Boy

Stormboy

Slugga Boy

Ork with converted big shoota.

The Warboss and his retinue mounted in a huge converted wartrukk.

SNAKEBITES

Snakebite Orks are distrustful of technology and prefer good old-fashioned stuff. Their warriors wear leather and furs for the most part, with some red and white markings.

Shoota Boy

Nob with big horns and bosspole.

These three Snakebites were made from bits from Warhammer 40,000 and Warhammer Orcs.

BAD MOONS

Bad Moons warbands are wealthy and well-equipped. Their ostentatious yellow clan colour is used as markings in a 'dog-tooth' pattern or as a background colour for black flames.

Nob with bosspole.

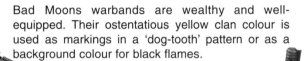

This wartrukk is fitted with a ram and a wrecker ball.

Slugga Boy

Stikk Bommas

Ork with converted rokkit launcha.

Nob with kustom shoota and bosspole.

DEATHSKULLS

Deathskull warbands are expert looters and scavengers and use blue as their clan colour, which most Orks think of as a lucky colour. Deathskulls often daub their bodies with blue warpaint to bring extra good fortune to their scavenging exploits.

Slugga Boys

BLOOD AXES

Blood Axe warbands are seen as being tainted by un-orky ideas picked up from human warriors on the battlefield and for this reason they are mistrusted by other Orks. Blood Axes often use camouflage colours, although they appear rather lurid to human eyes.

Shoota Boyz

EVIL SUNZ

Evil Sunz are obsessed with speed and love to ride in fast buggies. Their vehicles and warriors are all predominantly red (red ones go faster after all!), with some yellow detailing. Yellow flames are a common motif, and easy to paint too!

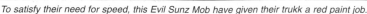

To satisfy their need for speed, this Evil Sunz Mob have given their trukk a red paint job.

FREEBOOTERS

Freebooter warbands are either made up of mobs of lots of different clans or mobs that don't belong to a clan at all. They don't care just as long as they are where the fighting is!

FREEBOOTERS

A Freebooter warband is an ideal opportunity to make up your own warband's colour scheme, so if you don't see any clan colours you like – go Freebooter! Many Freebooter warbands are an amalgam of Ork mobs from several different warbands. This means you could use a mix of Orks wearing different clan colours to give them a really rag-tag, undisciplined appearance.

Alternatively, you can create your own entirely original colour scheme – for example you might decide that Orks would look groovy in white (Snow Orks!) or grey. It's worth thinking about having a 'trademark' feature for your colour scheme (this is true of any warband, but especially Freebooters). For example the Bloodied Fist warband might have Orks which all have their fists painted red, whereas the Death Jawz have white jaws and so on.

This Nob has no specific clan glyphs or colours, the only decorations are a few checks and a lightning flash.

THEMED ARMIES

A themed army is one built around a single, distinctive idea. This might be a part of the background which appeals to you, or a style of play which you really like. For example, you might decide to collect a Goff warband around the idea that Goffs would never namby around with Wheelz, so the only vehicles you use are Ork Dreadnoughts: <u>lots</u> of Ork Dreadnoughts! Themed armies need a lot of planning, so they aren't very suitable if you're just starting out, but for an experienced gamer they are a great way of getting a unique and very personal force.

Adrian's Ork Nob wears white warpaint that distinguishes his Trukk mob, 'Da Dragsterz'.

ORK GLYPHS

Orks use glyphs to symbolise the important bits of their kultur, like violence, bloodshed and... more violence!

Clan Glyphs

Goff

Bad Moons

Deathskulls

Snakebites

Blood Axes

Evil Sunz

Nobz: Nobility, authority, high rank

Snikk: Cut, kill, execute, assassinate

Bad: Evil, bad, wicked, brave, strong, tough

Grim: Ruthless, prowess, face, dangerous

Zag: Lightning, movement, fast strike

Grub: Cunning, find, dig, hide

Skraga: Skarboy, veteran

Dakka: Attack, noisy weapon, shoot, fight

Gor: Blood, red, slaughter, wound

Boss: Leader, officer, head Ork, Warlord

Wazza: Speed, Kult of Speed

Regular Glyphs

Waaagh: Warband, tribe of, Watch Out!

Gull: Death, bones, skull, rocks, white

Orks mix and combine glyphs together to create new ones, for example the Blood Axes glyph has been combined with a skull. If a glyph represents something important like a Waaagh!, Orks make it really big. Glyphs are often made out of metal and can be painted too.

PAINTING DA WHEELZ

Ork armies often include a lot of Wheelz, because they're cheap and drive around much faster than the slower moving mass of Da Boyz. I always used to find painting vehicles daunting until I learned some good techniques...

Choose the colour you want to paint your vehicle and paint the whole model all over. If you decide to paint your vehicle Boltgun Metal, just drybrush the colour onto the black undercoated vehicle, it looks great immediately. After that, paint the wheels and the crew as normal and the vehicle is finished. You can add transfers at this point as well if you want to. Sorted!

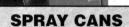

Ork warbike

SPRAY CANS

A very quick way to paint vehicles is to use spray cans. Simply choose the colour you want and either spray it over a black undercoat or directly onto the model (black is best though). You can also lightly dust the vehicle, using spray cans, over the base colour to make it look dirty or rusty. Afterwards drybrush on a lighter shade of your chosen base colour to bring the detail back out.

This wartrukk is fitted with a big grabber and painted in Boltgun Metal. You can use clan colours such as red and black if you like, to fit in with your army.

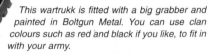

Big shoota	Rokkit launcha	Skorcha

Ork Dreadnought and Killer Kans

GUBBINZ

Ork vehicles are covered in bits and pieces commonly called 'gubbinz'. These bits can represent vehicle upgrades such as boarding planks and reinforced rams. However, more often than not gubbinz are either useful or decorative stuff that the crew have picked up, such as tools, trophies and fuel cans. Adding gubbinz is an easy way of modifying vehicles so that they don't all look the same.

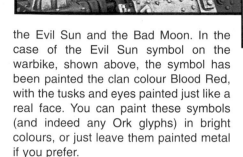

GLYPH PLATES

Ork miniatures and vehicles often feature clan symbols such as the Evil Sun and the Bad Moon. In the case of the Evil Sun symbol on the warbike, shown above, the symbol has been painted the clan colour Blood Red, with the tusks and eyes painted just like a real face. You can paint these symbols (and indeed any Ork glyphs) in bright colours, or just leave them painted metal if you prefer.

Transfers have been applied to this wartrak and drybrushed with Boltgun Metal to make them look as if the paint has been chipped away.

TRANSFERS

Transfers look great on both Ork miniatures and vehicles and there are loads of different designs to choose from. To apply waterslide transfers, carefully cut out the transfer and leave it in a saucer of water for 30 seconds. Using a pair of tweezers and a brush, slide the transfer off its backing paper and onto your model. Then use the corner of a tissue to dab away any excess water from the model and leave for a few minutes to let it dry completely. You can also combine transfers together to make new designs, re-paint them different colours or highlight them.

Checks have been painted onto this wartrak's sides, forks, and big shootas, as well as the gunner's wrist band. The areas to be painted with checks were undercoated Skull White first and then the grid was painted on in Chaos Black. Note the extensive battle damage to the armour plate on the front of the vehicle as well as to the mudguard.

DUST

Orks don't clean their vehicles, it's too much like hard work! Therefore buggies end up covered in dust and grime which is easy to paint onto your models. Just drybrush brown paint onto the vehicles or wheels and tracks.

In order to get transfers to stand out against metal body work, it's a good idea to paint a black background on first. When applied on top, white transfers stand out from the vehicle as shown with the flame effects on the front forks of this wartrak.

MEK'S WORKSHOP

One of the great things about Ork conversions is that you can make them as crude and as rough as you like!

The 'porthole' was made from a bit of a light fitting.

This wartrukk is festooned with armour plates made from metal and plastic Ork vehicle parts, as well as others created from plasti-card.

Andy used tank turrets to make the bodies for his Ork Dreadnoughts.

This wartrukk has had traks added, a remodelled hull and an impressive skorcha conversion.

CONVERTING VEHICLES

Vehicles are perfect for converting; it's relatively easy to make one buggy look very different from another. One way is to swop the front plate of a buggy for part of a trukk, or replace it with a metal front plates from another vehicle. There are loads of different bits and pieces for Ork vehicles that you can use to make a unique looking vehicle. If you are a bit more adventurous, you can really start swopping bits around, as you can see in the examples above. Extra wheels look good, as do additional weapons, battered armour plates, etc. We suggest that you also carve some battle damage into the plastic with a modelling knife or a pin vice drill.

You can even have a go at making your own Ork buildings. This one was made from a furniture drawer!

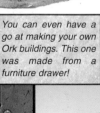

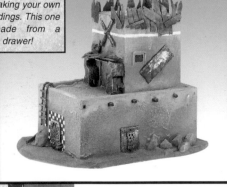

ORK STRONGHOLDS

Orks often construct makeshift strongholds for themselves and these pieces of scenery are an excellent addition to your battlefield. As you can see above, there are already a fort and a stronghold available as card buildings. If you want, you can also add parts from the Battlefield Accessory set such as barrels and tank traps.

PAINTING TIPS

This page details lots of different tips that you will find useful for painting Orks. Look out for more in *White Dwarf* magazine.

BATTLE DAMAGE

Battleworn paint over metal looks great on Ork miniatures and is very easy to do. We used this effect on this Ork's shoulder armour. After painting the armour red, random shapes were painted onto it in Chaos Black. Then Boltgun Metal was painted over the black areas leaving a slight line of black showing. To finish it off, a little Mithril Silver can be painted on to make the metal look really worn.

PAINTING CHECKS

Painting checks onto models and vehicles is simple once you know how. Start by painting the area you want the check pattern on with Skull White (or any other light colour). Then paint parallel lines horizontally and vertically in Chaos Black to make a grid. Finally paint alternate squares to create a chequered effect.

WARPAINT

One of the best ways to unify your mobs of Orks is warpaint. Choose the colour for the mob and paint marks onto the skin. Ork glyphs look good, as well as simple lines and dags. If the mob belongs to a particular clan, such as an Evil Sunz mob, use warpaint in the appropriate clan colour, in this case red.

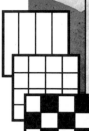

DAGS

Also called dog-tooth pattern, dags are a good Orky decoration for both troops and vehicles. First paint a zig-zag pattern and then fill in each alternate triangle.

ORK CONVERSIONS

Individual Orks are just as much fun to convert as their vehicles.

Plastic Orks are perfect for converting, there are so many different combinations that you can really let your imagination run riot. Swapping arms, weapons and heads is the easiest way to change a figure. For instance, adding plates to their front, back and shoulders is a good way of making 'Ard Boyz.

Adrian Wood's crazy Storm Boy conversion.

Note the extra bolts and glyph trimmed off and glued onto this 'Ard Boy.

Brian Nelson's superbly simple conversion features the human head from the Ork sprue.

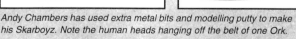

Andy Chambers has used extra metal bits and modelling putty to make his Skarboyz. Note the human heads hanging off the belt of one Ork.

Both these Deathskull Lootas are armed with Space Marine heavy weapons. These conversions are very simple: just cut off the shootas and add the Imperial guns.

This dynamically posed Ork is one of Dave Gallagher's conversions. The legs have been cut to create a headlong charge.

Dave's Ork with big shoota was made by adding an extra barrel length to the shoota and repositioning the legs and feet to get a recoil effect.

BIG TOOF RIVER

The Battle of Big Toof river was created as a display for Games Day '97. Ork fanatics throughout Games Workshop contributed hundreds of figures to create this truly awe-inspiring spectacle.

▲ *A scratch built Ork Fighta Bomma swoops over the battlefield.*

The huge Ork fort dominates one corner of Big Toof river. You can see mob after mob of the Ork defenders pouring onto the battlefield.

Can you spot the Vindicare Assassin? ▶

One of the centre pieces of the whole display is this enormous Gargant built from card, tubing and lots (and lots!) of scavenged bits from kits and other models.

Countless buggies sweep over the hill and onto the Imperial positions.

▶The Stormboyz jump Big Toof river in order to assault the Imperial Guard defenders.

◀ Leading one of the columns of Orks through the outlying Ork buildings is this huge scratch-built Squiggoth.

 ◀ ▲

Captured Imperial vehicles kustomised by the Mekaniaks strike out for the Imperial Tank forces.

SHOWCASE

On this page are some of the best Ork models that we've ever seen. The Golden Demon painting competition at Games Day always features loads of great Orky conversions!

Nigel Carman converted his own Ghazghkull Thraka.

Andy Chambers' Waaagh! banner Nob.

Ork Dreadnought by *José Antonio Romero.*

Steve Buddle won the best Warhammer 40,000 Vehicle category at Golden Demon '97 with this imaginative looted Imperial vehicle.

Adrian Wood's scratch-built battlewagon.

ORKS

This next part of the Codex is given over to all the bits and pieces that don't form part of the army list or hobby guide. This includes rules for new weapons and wargear detailed in the Ork Armoury and a selection of infamous Ork Warbosses and warriors to use as special characters in your games. In addition to these we have compiled a series of treatises and studies about the Ork race which continues to plague the Imperium. Hopefully these should be of some interest to players who are running campaigns or want to create their own clans and warbands – as well as being a good laugh of course!

TRANSMITTED: Midal II
RECEIVED: Genneman Prime
DESTINATION: Mars
DATE: 6738374.M41
TELEPATHIC DUCT:
Astropath-terminus Melial
REF: AdMech/01159168298/GW
AUTHOR: Magos Biologis Rastex
TITLE: Preface: Growth patterns of Orks in variant societies

It is widely accepted as fact that prolonged periods of conflict lead to an increase in the size and strength of Orkoid individuals. Our research team set out to investigate whether this phenomenon had additional, further reaching, effects on Ork societies. We have spent the last two decades studying Ork communities in various regions of the Segmentum Obscurus, taking physical samples and comparing their exological composition. The evidence we have gathered is highly conclusive.

Orkoid settlements which have undergone long term isolation, with relatively few Orks [up to 10,000] show a decline in size and stature from those more regularly encountered. Samples taken from Ork colonies in the Paramar and Goliant Sectors, where Orks are low in density, showed a decrease in body mass of 15–19%. They were less physically aggressive [although still capable of tearing a man limb from limb if necessary]. To compensate for this reduction of stature, greater reliance is placed on their crude technology, with ranged fighting taking greater precedence over the brutal affair of close mêlée. This sub-type of Ork is not widely found, both due to the fact that such developments take place in the most solitary and backwater conditions.

Conversely, Orks in greater numbers are much more likely to be fiercer in combat; more aggressive and short tempered; impatient and less likely to employ ranged weaponry with any noticeable effect. It appears that the greater the number of Orks present [on a global and interplanetary scale] the more the Orks' savage basic instincts prevail. Such specimens are physically larger than their scattered counterparts, and the muscle:mass ratio of their exological make-up is greater [in other words there is literally strength in numbers for the Orks].

Attempts to penetrate the so-called Ork enclaves of Gathrog and Dregruk in the southern regions of the Segmentum have proved unsuccessful. The Orks have dominated these areas unchecked since before the founding of the Imperium and it is, quite reasonably, surmised that within an area of only a few light years there are tens of millions of the creatures. It is possible that in such conditions the Orks' physical proportions are even more pronounced, with whole planetary populations the size of the sub-type known to our warriors as 'Skarboyz'. When one considers the size of the 'Nobz' and 'Warbosses' of even relatively small Ork armies, one shudders to think of the monstrous creatures that must dominate these cultures. Should ever such a monster be filled with a desire for conquest, it is a matter of much debate whether any military means at our disposal could stop them.

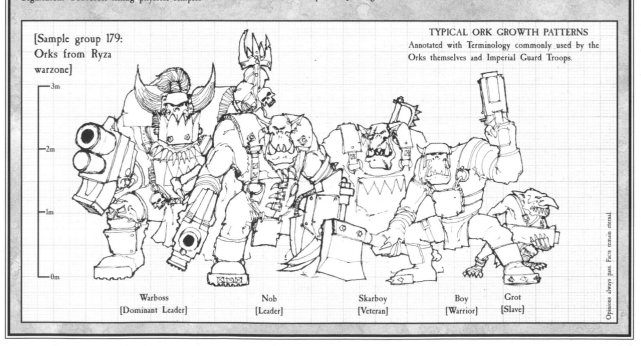

[Sample group 179: Orks from Ryza warzone]

TYPICAL ORK GROWTH PATTERNS
Annotated with Terminology commonly used by the Orks themselves and Imperial Guard Troops.

| Warboss [Dominant Leader] | Nob [Leader] | Skarboy [Veteran] | Boy [Warrior] | Grot [Slave] |

Opinions always pass. Facts remain eternal.

ORK WARGEAR

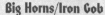

The following rules describe how all of the specialised equipment used by Orks works during a battle. These rules tend to be more detailed than those in the Warhammer 40,000 rulebook, and supersede them if they are different. Anything not listed here functions exactly as described in the Warhammer 40,000 rulebook.

Ammo Runt

An ammo runt is a heavily overburdened Gretchin who carries a massive amount of extra ammo for his master. One Ork model in base-to-base contact with an ammo runt in the shooting phase is allowed to re-roll one To Hit dice. The ammo runt is removed once the re-roll has been used – it can be imagined that the runt has gone running back to camp to fetch more ammo for his master (but with typical Grot slovenliness will not return during the battle!).

An ammo runt may not be chosen as a casualty caused by enemy shooting (they stay well out of the way 'cos they're carrying lots of ammo!) but Blast markers and template weapons will affect them as normal. Ammo runts removed because they are 'used up' do not count for morale or victory points purposes.

	WS	BS	S	T	W	I	A	Ld	Sv
Ammo Runt	2	2	2	2	1	2	1	5	–

Attack Squig

Some varieties of squig are vicious predators with razor sharp fangs or a poisonous bite. Attack squigs are specially trained to accompany an Ork character and attack the enemy on command. They have the following characteristics:

	WS	BS	S	T	W	I	A	Ld	Sv
Attack Squig	3	0	3	3	1	4	2	3	6+

Choppa

Beloved of Ork Nobz in particular, choppas are usually immense axe-like weapons or brutal cleavers. Choppas frequently have a chainsaw edge to make them extra rippy when it comes to chopping through armour. In close combat choppas limit the saving throw an enemy model can have to a 4+ at best. So, for example, if a Space Marine in power armour or Terminator armour were hit and wounded by an Ork with a choppa they would have to roll a 4 or more to make their saving throw.

Big Horns/Iron Gob

Ork leaders commonly display their prowess by hunting down and killing dangerous beasts. The creatures they fight against the most are those with big horns or tusks which can then be displayed on the Nob's helmet for all the Boyz to see. If such a creature has a disappointing lack of horns or tusks the Ork leader will sport a huge metal jaw instead to show that he has got the biggest bite around! If a mob is led by a Warboss or Nob with either Big Horns or an Iron Gob they add +1 to their Leadership value. Note that the two may not be combined to get a +2 bonus.

Bionik Arm

Ork bioniks are typically crude but effective. Ork bionik arms are equipped with built-in weapons as standard – be they one-shot sluggas, retractable spikes, ferocious creatures in cages or something even more unsubtle. An Ork with a bionik arm causes one automatic Strength 4 hit in close combat with the equivalent of Initiative 6, but only if in base-to-base contact with the target. The plethora of spikes, blades and other hurty bits welded on to the arm mean it also counts as an additional close combat weapon. This may not be combined with mega armour.

Bionik Bonce

Orks with serious head injuries may well come back from the Mad Dok's with most of their cranium replaced by solid armour plates. An Ork with a bionik bonce adds +1 to its armour saving throw. This may not be combined with mega armour.

Bosspole

In addition to their Big Horns and Iron Gobs, successful Nobz have a trophy pole to carry interesting souvenirs from foes they have defeated in battle. The pole may be carried by the Nob (strapped to his back) or by a member of his mob (including a Grot but not a squig). An Ork mob trying to mob up with a mob carrying a bosspole may re-roll their Leadership test if they fail on the first try.

Burna

Burnas are cutting torches used by Mekboyz for carving up vehicle wrecks into useable chunks. However, a quick twist of the mixture valve and WHOOOSH! the burna spits out a blast of incinerating flames. A burna may be fired in the shooting phase with the stats shown below or in close combat as a power weapon. It may not be used to shoot and fight in close combat within the same turn. Burnas roll 2D6 instead of 1D6 for armour penetration against vehicles.

Range	Str	AP	Notes
Template	4	5	Assault 1

Cybork Body

Critically injured Orks may survive to fight again after an extensive rebuild at the Mad Dok's. An Ork with a Cybork body can survive terrible injuries and so gains a 5+ invulnerable saving throw.

Dok's Tools

A Mad Dok with Dok's tools can have a go at 'fixin' one wounded Ork in the mob he is in each turn at the end of his enemy's shooting phase, even Orks reduced to zero wounds can be saved... perhaps! If several Orks have been wounded the Mad Dok can choose which to assist. Roll a D6 for his efforts and look up the result below.

D6   Result

1   **Aaargh!** The Ork suffers 1 wound. If reduced to zero wounds, remove the Ork as a casualty.

2-5   **Da patient is restin'....** The Dok achieves precisely nothing this time. If the Ork had been reduced to zero wounds remove it as a casualty.

6   **Job's a good 'un!** The Ork regains 1 wound, up to the maximum it started the game with.

'Eavy Armour

Ork 'eavy armour is made up of thick armour plates shaped to fit an Ork (sort of) and cover up its few vulnerable spots. This gives the Ork wearing it a 4+ armour save.

Grabba Stik

Grabba stiks are long catchpoles that Slaverz use to catch wayward Grots. In close combat a Slaver armed with a grabba stik can make its full number of attacks even if it is 2" away from an enemy model. The stik's effects may not be combined with any other special close combat weapons or attacks.

Grot Orderly

Mad Doks often have a small gaggle of Gretchin slaves that help fetch and carry, stitch wounds, etc. Each orderly in base-to-base contact with a Mad Dok gives him a +1 bonus on the dice roll for using Dok's tools, up to a max of +3. However the Grot's enthusiasm often exceeds its capabilities so a roll of 1 before bonuses always fails and inflicts a wound on the unfortunate patient.

	WS	BS	S	T	W	I	A	Ld	Sv
Grot orderly	2	2	2	2	1	2	1	5	–

Grot Oiler

Mekboyz use Grot slaves to carry their tools, hold stuff in place, bash in extra nails, etc. Each Grot oiler in base-to-base contact with a Mekboy gives them a +1 bonus to the dice roll for using their Mek's tools, up to a maximum of +3. Grot oilers sometimes get under the Mek's feet and pull the wrong wires out so a roll of 1 always fails.

	WS	BS	S	T	W	I	A	Ld	Sv
Grot Oiler	2	2	2	2	1	2	1	5	–

Kannon

Kannon are heavy guns mounted on wheeled carriages and crewed by Gretchin. They can fire either a big bore frag round for blasting infantry or a solid shell for punching through tanks. They are appallingly inaccurate but make very, very big holes when they hit!

Kannon may use frag or shell rounds: choose which you are firing with before rolling to hit. Frag rounds are resolved in the same way as ordnance but use the small Blast marker – place the marker (within range and line of sight) and roll the Scatter dice and a D6. The marker moves D6" in the direction indicated if an arrow is rolled. If a 'hit' is rolled the shot lands on target but if a 6 is rolled on the D6 a hit is scored and one of the Gretchin krew is killed in a nasty firing accident. Kannons firing shells roll to hit as normal and have a BS of 2.

Against vehicles shells count as an ordnance hit, so roll 2D6 for armour penetration and pick the highest results. Any penetrating hits roll for damage on the Ordnance Damage table, for glancing hits use the Glancing Hits table as normal. Kannon have the following characteristics:

	Range	Str	AP	Notes
Kannon (Frag)	36"	5	5	Heavy 1/Blast
Kannon (Shell)	36"	8	3	Heavy 1

Kombi-Weapons

A kombi-weapon is two weapons nailed/wired/welded together, and gives the Ork a choice of two weapons to fire with. An Ork that is armed with a kombi-weapon may choose to fire one of the weapons during the shooting phase. The shoota may be fired any number of times, but the other weapon is only allowed to be fired once per battle. Note that you may not choose to fire both of these weapons at the same time. A kombi-weapon may be upgraded with kustom jobs but the customising only applies to the shoota part of the weapon.

Kustom Mega-Blasta

A kustom mega-blasta is a marvel of Ork technology which works by firing a blast of energy at the target. However, if a mega-blasta rolls a 1 To Hit it scores a wound on the Ork carrying it (normal armour saves apply) or scores a glancing hit on the vehicle carrying it.

Range	Str	AP	Notes
24"	7	2	Heavy 1/Blast/gets hot!

Kustom Force Field

Mekboyz have an uncanny understanding of battlefield technology and will sometimes build or scavenge powerful force field projectors to protect the Boyz on the battlefield.

A kustom force field gives all models within 6" a 5+ cover saving throw, vehicles within 6" are treated as being hull down. The force field has no effect in close combat.

Kustom Job: More Dakka

Mekboyz spend much of their time tinkering with weaponry to make it more powerful or faster to fire. More Dakka kustomisin' makes a shoota or slugga Assault 2 instead of rapid fire or pistol respectively (More Dakka sluggas may still be used in close combat however). A More Dakka kustom job may be combined with a Shootier kustom job to produce a S5, assault 2 shoota or slugga.

Kustom Job: Shootier

Just as popular as More Dakka kustom jobs, Shootier weapons use a larger calibre and heavier ammo to give them more punch. A Shootier kustom job makes a shoota or slugga S5 instead of S4.

Kustom Job: Blasta

A shoota or slugga with the Blasta kustom job has extra heavy duty armour piercing ammo or is radically altered so that it fires a lethal energy bolt capable of burning through armour. A Blasta kustom job gives a shoota or slugga AP3 at up to 12" range, increasing to AP2 if the target is within 6". But a shoota or slugga with the Blasta kustom job gets hot just like a plasma weapon, so on a roll of 1 To Hit the weapon scores a wound on its firer; normal armour saves apply.

Lobba

These are artillery pieces crewed by Gretchin. They are called lobbas because they 'lob' their payload in a high arc onto the enemy. How they go about lobbing their munitions varies. Most look like big mortars or howitzers but rockets are popular too and there have even been reports of medieval-style catapults and trebuchets being used. Regardless of their type all lobbas work in the same way as standard barrage weapons – guess range and roll for scatter. However if a 'Hit' and a 6 are rolled together a hit is scored but one of the Lobba's Gretchin krew is killed in an unfortunate mishap (launched high into the air, crushed by the Lobba's recoil, etc).

Range	Str	AP	Notes
Guess 48"	5	5	Heavy 1/Blast

Mega Armour

Mega armour is a suit of massively thick and heavy armour plates over a powered exo-skeleton. Though slow mega armour has the advantages of giving a 2+ armour save and includes a shoota and power claw. However, an Ork in mega armour always moves as if in difficult terrain (but there's no extra penalty if actually moving through difficult terrain). If you have a unit that includes several Orks with mega armour just make one roll to see how far the Orks get. Mega armour weaponry may not be changed for other types (because it's built in) but the shoota may be upgraded to a kombi-shoota and/or a kustom shoota. An Ork in mega armour may not use the following abilities, equipment or weapons: *jump packs, bikes, infiltration, bioniks, frag or krak stikkbombz or tankbusta bombz.*

Ref: AdMech/0115242004/GW
Author: Genetor Lukas Anzion
Title: Chapter XVII: Genetic predetermination – Hereditary skill acquisition within the Ork caste and professional social structure.

It has long been known that the psychological aspects of a human is, in part, determined by their genetic heritage. Certain geno-types are disposed towards pre-determined personality traits which, in turn, informs the process of learning and aptitude. In Orks this genetic predetermination is also present, though in a different and even more pronounced fashion. It appears that not only is aptitude towards certain aspects of the culture present in the gene-structure, actual skills and knowledge are also encoded into the genetic strand.

The best analogy one can think of is to compare this knowledge with the basic motor skills present in a human child. A human child does not have to be taught how to breathe, how to make its heart beat or how to employ the many thousands of other biological functions that are already operating at the time of birth. In a similar way, an Ork predisposed towards science and mechanics [Meks] has an encoded knowledge of basic physics and mechanical engineering theory. However, this knowledge is as subconscious as the baby's ability to breathe; it is an unconscious competence in whatever field the individual is created for. In the same way that a child can learn to alter their breathing, hold their breath or, through exercise, improve the capacity of their lungs and vascular system, so too can an Ork build upon these innate skills through the normal process of learning. The two major skill groups created in this fashion are the castes known as Doks and Meks.

Doks are the Orkoid medical experts, who have a rough and ready knowledge of Orkoid xenological composition. Due to the hardiness of Ork physiognomy, Ork surgical and medical techniques are as crude but effective as the rest of their technology. Wounds can be easily stitched tight with wire or stapled, while broken bones need little in the way of setting to speed the healing process. Internal injuries are similarly treated, and the multiple redundancy of many Ork organs also provides plenty of transplant donors for those in need of such measures [although the donation is not always made voluntarily, particularly where the casualty is an important member of the society]. Orks are generally loathe to undergo medical treatment.

This is for two reasons. Firstly, many Orks consider such an activity as a sign of weakness, and there is a strong compulsion throughout Ork society for natural selection to take its course – the weak must die out so that the spores of the stronger may thrive and grow into stronger Orks. Secondly, the gene-determination of Doks imbues them with a highly active curiosity, coupled with a callous disregard for the well-being of those they treat. Many Doks see surgery and treatment as a means for experimentation upon their patient, and often Orks undergo horrendous and entirely unnecessary surgical procedures to satisfy the Dok's inquisitiveness or as a trial for a new procedure of prosthetic. Such treatments are not tested in any scientific manner before their employment and horribly disabling injuries can result from such procedures.

Meks are similarly driven to experimentation, although in the field of mechanical rather than medical science. Much of the weaponry and wargear used by the Orks, as well as more mundane artefacts, are designed and built by the Meks. As much of their knowledge is subconscious, the vast majority of Meks never truly understand what they are creating, or the exact functions of how they work. As Orks are poor rationalists, this can lead to rather unlikely conventions.

For example, it is widely believed by Orks that machines painted in a red colour operate faster. This could have come about by the following situation. A Mek builds two vehicles which, as far as it is aware of, are exactly the same except for the fact that one is painted red and the other yellow. However, due to some unseen variation in fuel, lubrication, or some other factor, the red vehicle in fact travels faster. To the Ork, the only conceivable explanation for this is that the vehicle travels faster because it is red.

However, as disturbing as it sounds, these 'facts' become true. Red Ork vehicles do travel perceptibly faster than those of other colours, even when all other design aspects are nominally the same. Similarly, many captured Ork weapons and items of equipment should not work, and indeed do not work unless wielded by an Ork. I believe this is linked to the strong psychic aura surrounding all Orkoids and have developed the Anzion Theorem of Orkoid Mechamorphic Resonant Kinetics. I theorise that many Ork inventions work because the Orks themselves think that they should work. The strong telekinetic abilities of the Orks' subconscious somehow ensure that the machinery or weaponry functions as desired.

As astounding as it may be, we cannot make any other conclusion based on the evidence to hand.

Orkses is never beaten in battle. If we win we win, if we die we die so it don't count as beat. If we runs for it we don't die neither, so we can always come back for anuvver go, see!

Anon